ENCOUNTER GOD

CLAIRE ELIZABETH GROSE

Copyright © 2024 by Claire Elizabeth Grose

Compiled and edited by Michael Grose and June Kennedy

All rights reserved. No portion of this publication may be reproduced, stored in a retrieval system or transmitted in any form by any means – electronic, mechanical, photocopying, recording, or any other –except for brief quotation in printed reviews, without the prior written permission of the publisher.

Unless indicated otherwise, all scripture quotations in this book are from the following source:

The Good News Bible: The Bible in Today's English Version (TEV) © 1976 by the American Bible Society. Used with permission.

ISBN 978-0-6459888-2-6

Author contact information - clairegrose.heartmatters@gmail.com

Version 1.0

DEDICATION

This book is dedicated to Costa
My beloved Grandson

CONTENTS

DEDICATION	IV
CONTENTS	V
PREFACE	VIII
ACKNOWLEDGEMENTS	X
PART ONE	1
MY DAILY PRAYER	4
REVELATION BREAKTHROUGH	5
PERFECT PEACE	6
SUSTAINING LOVE	7
THE BLESSING OF YOUR LOVE	8
FRESH SEA BREEZE	9
PURE JOY	10
PLEASURES IN HIS CREATION	11
BLUE OF NIGHT	14
BLESSINGS WILL COME	15
A LOVE TO TREASURE	16
I NEED YOU BY MY SIDE	17
HOLY SPIRIT'S PROMPTS	18
HIS LOVE COMES QUIETLY	19
GOLDEN FRIENDSHIPS	20
FEEDING ON GOD'S LOVE	21
EXCITEMENT IN MY SOUL	22
A LOVE THAT KNOWS NO END	23
IN SERVICE FOR VICTORY	26
KNOW HIM LIKE A BROTHER	27
A LOVE THAT KNOWS NO BOUNDS	28
AMONGST YOUR BEAUTY LORD	29
PART TWO	30
ONWARD AS I AM	33
TRUST IN THEE	34
TREASURES IN YOUR LOVE	35
ALL IS NOT LOST	36

TEARS WILL SLIP AWAY	*37*
SURROUND YOURSELF WITH GOD	*38*
PRAY FOR PEACE AND CALM	*41*
LOOK TO THE HOLY SPIRIT	*42*
PERSONAL TIME WITH THE SAVIOUR	*43*
NEVER ALONE	*44*
LOOK TO THE SAVIOUR	*45*
LIVE HIS WORD EVERYDAY	*46*
IN YOUR LOVING CARE	*49*
LORD IN YOU	*50*
I NEED YOUR DIRECTION LORD	*51*
HIS CALM IS YOUR CALM	*52*
HIS LOVE WILL SUSTAIN YOU	*53*
FIND PEACE WITH THE SAVIOUR	*54*
COME INTO HIS SANCTUARY	*57*
CHALLENGES	*58*
SHINING ON THE INSIDE	*59*
BRAVE HEARTED	*60*
EMPOWERING LOVE	*61*
BLESSED BY YOUR SPIRIT	*62*
YOUR PRESENCE ALONE	*63*
THRONE OF GLORY	*64*
FLOURISHING LOVE	*65*
TALK TO THE HOLY SPIRIT	*66*
SALVATION IS AT HAND	*67*
SPIRIT HOME	*68*
PART THREE	*69*
SO FAITHFUL	*72*
BECAUSE OF YOU LORD	*73*
ALONE WITH MY THOUGHTS	*74*
HEAVEN'S LANDSCAPE	*75*
GIFT DIVINE	*76*
FULFILMENT	*77*
AWAKENING OF THE SPIRIT	*80*
IN LOVE WITH JESUS	*81*

- HIS MIRACLES HAPPEN TODAY 82
- PEACE FOR REST 83
- OPEN TO THE SPIRIT 84
- MY SOUL'S DELIGHT 85
- PART FOUR 86
  - WORSHIP AND SONG 89
  - HEAVEN'S KEY 90
  - REACHING ARMS 91
  - THE GLORY OF GOD'S POWER 94
  - GLORIOUS EASTER DAY 95
  - GOD'S FAVOUR POURED OUT 98
  - HOLY, HOLY NIGHT 99
  - A LOVE SO REAL 100
  - ALWAYS AND FOREVER 101

PREFACE

Two things I just wanted to say about this book are, why I started writing and how I came by the title.

I grew up in the 1950's-1960's in Adelaide, South Australia, my life was pretty simple but wonderful. I was very lucky to have a secure family life, and my Mum and Dad brought the family up to treat others with respect, do the right thing, be courteous, and respect your elders. We had a strict upbringing and even as adults our parents never criticized us but encouraged us to do our best in life. They were "Aussie battlers" but we always managed to make it through the tough times!

They were people of integrity and cared about others and instilled that into our family.

Church was a big part of our lives growing up. We went to Sunday School at an early age and progressed up through the appropriate groups as we got older.

Youth groups, camps and church anniversaries were all important to the whole family. We competed in church sports teams, basketball and tennis with other parishes across Adelaide. Life-long friendships were in the making and cherished golden memories to look back on that would never fade.

Bible stories, hymns and choruses were all part of getting to know Jesus. This nurturing finally led me to the day Jesus came knocking on my heart's door. Being filled with the Holy Spirit is something I will never forget and the overwhelming power of His love that filled my whole being and propelled me to the front of the hall to give my heart to Him. No words can fully describe the joy I felt. That was in February 1968, I was 14 years of age. He has been my Shining Light ever since, and lives within me always.

So I thank my beautiful Mum and Dad for the way they raised me and for the foundation of knowing Jesus' love.

It was in His love that I started to write, in the autumn of 1993. My journey has brought me to this book " Encounter God", my 12th book. The title came to me thinking of encountering God every day of my life and how much comfort and peace I have found in His Word and His companionship day by day.

To Encounter God means taking that step to commune with The Almighty God, The Everlasting Father, The Prince of Peace in all aspects of every day life. He comes by invitation with the blessing of The Holy Spirit who dwells in each heart who believes, bringing God's peace, calm and great love. You only have to confess that you believe Jesus died on the Cross to gain forgiveness for the world's sin and was raised to everlasting life by His Heavenly Father and sits at His right hand in Heaven.

Luke 24:7, Acts 2:33 - Good News Bible.

When I was a young Christian reading my Bible was really important to me in getting to know Jesus as my personal Saviour and became the foundation that I built my faith on.

It gave me strength and courage as I began life in the workforce at the age of 16. Coming from a sheltered upbringing it was my life-line to self-confidence and adapting to social life at work.
The poems reflect the everyday feelings and emotions that we feel as we meet the challenges of life and how the great magnitude of God's love can help us rise above them.

Many of these writings have been my first words of whispered prayer, so much that I have been moved to write them down at once and continue on in His wonderful and absolute love.

Together we write as He provides my inspiration.

All glory to Him, my precious Lord Jesus!

ACKNOWLEDGEMENTS

My heartfelt thanks to my beloved family, my Mum and Dad, Lilly and Ken, and my siblings Jeanette, June, Carol, Gloria and Lynne, for their never ending encouragement and support to me. To the rest of the family, you are all a precious link that joins us together.

To Michael and Andrew for your continual support to me in fulfilling my passion of writing poems for the Lord to help others through His Word.

A huge thank you to Junie for editing my poems and the coffees and lunches we enjoyed along the way.

To Joy Furnell for her Crown of Thorns drawing, you have an amazing gift, thank you Joy.

A special thank you to Salisbury Uniting Church, Adelaide for photos. Used by permission.

A big thank you to Carol, Dennis, Karen, Jeff, and Kate for great photos.

To my friends and Church Families, thank you for your love and support.

To my beautiful sons, Michael and Andrew, and your Partners and my Grandchildren. Thank you for loving me, and I am so glad He gave you to me. I will love you all forever.

To you the reader, thank you for picking this book up and I pray you will find His peace and love on the pages ahead.

May He shower you all with His love and blessings.

PART ONE

"Christ is the visible likeness of the invisible God. He is the first-born Son, superior to all created things. For through him God created everything in heaven and on earth, the seen and the unseen things, including spiritual powers, lords, rulers, and authorities. God created the whole universe through him and for him."

Colossians 1 : 15, 16

ENCOUNTER GOD

HIS MOST LOVED CREATION...
IS YOU...

"He is the key that opens all the hidden treasures of God's wisdom and knowledge."

Colossians 2 : 3

MY DAILY PRAYER

Be with me, stay with me,
Close by my side,
Fill me with Your peace and love,
So my spirit shall surely fly
To the heights in Your love,
As only You can give,
Prepare me for this day ahead,
So in me You'll always live.

REVELATION BREAKTHROUGH

Your heart revelation breakthrough
Is victory indeed,
The Holy Spirit takes His place,
God's precious Holy Seed.

A resurgence of the heart
Now it's open wide,
The Spirit's flame ignites
A love you just can't hide.

A feeling of cleansing
Now you've encountered God,
No chance meeting;
His wings you ride upon.

Your revelation breakthrough,
In praise angels roar,
Your name is known in heaven,
In the Spirit's love you soar.

Such power and wonder you know,
A child of the Most High,
Your revelation breakthrough
Has forever changed your life!

PERFECT PEACE

Perfect peace is what I feel
When I trust in You,
My faith and love so strong,
It's all I need to do.

When I feel worried
And fear rises up,
I cling to You Lord,
God's own precious Son.

I have no doubt at all
That You will look after me,
In You I claim my prayer
Because of Calvary.

I have perfect peace,
Calmness I feel,
My trust in You secure,
My love for You so real.

Your Spirit brought Your peace to me,
He is Your precious gift,
I thank You Holy Father
Because in me He lives.

SUSTAINING LOVE

Thank You Lord
For Your love that sustains,
Through all things
When we are open to Your ways.

We are never too far
From Your reach,
Though life overwhelms
Our prayers You still seek.

Your sustaining love
Knows no bounds,
In Your tender loving care
Our faith is sound.

Your sustaining love Lord
Comes from eternity,
Forever it flows
From You to me.

Your sustaining love so powerful
From centuries ago,
Is a love that sustains us
That will never let us go!

THE BLESSING OF YOUR LOVE

The blessing of Your love Lord
Is for all the world,
Each one You made unique
With Your love that overwhelms.

For every open heart
You have the gift of life,
To all who will receive
Your power and Your light.

In the realms of heaven Lord
You live in glory and light,
The blessings of Your love Lord
Make us precious in Your sight.

The blessing of Your love Lord
Will see eternity,
Forever and always Lord
You will be our Majesty.

FRESH SEA BREEZE

The waves roll to the shore
In relentless harmony,
Each one in rhythm
As I gaze upon the sea.

Grey seems all around,
Sky's reflection on the sea,
But I hear Your voice
Bringing peace to me.

I love it Lord when I feel Your peace
Your joy will never fade,
Coming to me on the beach,
Sea breeze upon my face.

Rejuvenation of my soul
As freshness spurs me on,
I can face another day,
Restored, I move along.

To You the sea was no different
To the ground You walked upon,
Just as much Your home,
You; The Son of God.

PURE JOY

Pure joy, my Saviour,
That's what He gives to me,
Through His Holy Spirit,
Happy I can be.

There is no other way
To know God's Holy Love;
Shining on the inside
When you feel the Spirit's love.

When I surrender to Him
And share my every need,
Through trust and faith
I know He lives in me.

I know pure joy,
From the Saviour above,
Because I opened my heart
To the King of Love!

PLEASURES IN HIS CREATION

Find pleasures in His creation
As far as the eye can see,
In power and glory it evolved
To supply all our needs.

His beauty is all around us,
In sight, smell and touch,
There's pleasure in His creation
That we love so very much.

Awe and wonder we find
As we seek out His world,
The stars come out at night
To purely overwhelm.

There's pleasure in His creation,
More than we will ever understand,
Take time to enjoy it,
Part of His Holy plan.

LITTLE STEPS OF FAITH...
BECOME BIG ONES...

"How great are God's riches!
How deep are his wisdom and knowledge!
Who can explain his decisions?
Who can explain His ways?"

Romans 11 : 33

BLUE OF NIGHT

Blue of night as dusk rolls in
While sun prepares to bow,
Earth keeps on revolving
As evening enters now.

Blue of night calls the stars
Set by the Saviour's hand,
Made from His creation
Called on the Father's command.

The heat of day has passed now,
Showers refresh the fading light,
Revive the thirst of day,
Now comes the blue of night.

Blue of night calls rest,
Moon shines high above,
Constellations take their place,
Encounter God's glorious love.

The ebb of the tide keeps rolling
In the blue of night,
Father God is in His heaven
While we rest 'til morning light.

BLESSINGS WILL COME

His blessings will come
To those unbeknown,
To strengthen and guide
Your pathway shown.

Take in His beauty
With every dawn and dusk,
They will bring you joy
And His blessings will come.

Encounter God in many ways,
To feel His presence near,
Take a moment to stop
And watch the shadows clear.

Mother Nature a glory,
Wonders all around,
Everywhere all over the earth
His creation is found.

His blessings will come
Because He loves us so,
At any given time, just call,
You are never alone.

A LOVE TO TREASURE

A love to treasure
Belongs to the Lord,
It first was His,
Now it's mine to adore.

He came to me
A long time ago,
When my journey was steep
And my footsteps were slow.

A love so pure
With riches to embrace,
Arms always open
Full of mercy and grace.

A love that knows forgiveness
For every sin,
A home for each stranger
Who welcomes Him in.

A passion so strong
Drove Him to Calvary,
The price so high,
One life rose to victory.

A love to treasure
Will never let me go,
A love to treasure
Just grows and grows.

I NEED YOU BY MY SIDE

Thank You Lord for Your presence today,
I need You by my side,
Bless this day today
As the hours pass on by.

In every minute of the day,
I need You by my side,
No matter how small or large,
My need You recognize.

I revere You Mighty Lord
And Your help for today,
In asking for Your strength
My faith is displayed.

I need You by my side Lord,
Dear Heavenly Father above,
Today and every day
I call on You for love.

HOLY SPIRIT'S PROMPTS

A love that makes you give
Without knowing why,
A love so real
In your heart will abide.

A prompt you felt
From The Spirit so real,
Will change your thinking
And the way you feel.

When you listen to The Spirit
And give Him some time,
This encounter with God
Will make you shine.

Life will still present
Its challenges some days,
But His love so real inside you
Will pave the way.

HIS LOVE COMES QUIETLY

I love the way You come to me,
I know it's surely You,
You fill me with Your love divine,
I know this is true.

When I'm sitting quietly
Or drifting off to sleep,
You come to my mind,
Comfort is what I seek.

You have my full attention,
My prayers I whisper to You,
Assurance I know completely
As I confess my cares to You.

Your love comes so quietly,
Peace and calm I know,
Your Spirit is Your messenger
Because Your love He shows.

I feel renewed in Your love
As I leave my trust in You,
Your love comes quietly
And makes me feel brand new.

GOLDEN FRIENDSHIPS

Golden friendships mellow in time
Through trust you cannot buy,
In open hearts of love
The ones the Saviour provides.

Sharing a path in the journey of life
That the Lord planned long ago,
No burden is too heavy
As your trust and faith will show.

These are no chance meetings,
Unconditional love rules the day,
The Saviour knows our needs,
His Spirit will show us the way.

Golden friendships just keep on growing
When The Spirit comes to bless,
An anointing of such peace
From The Silent, Unseen Guest.

Golden friendships are such a comfort,
Joys can be shared by two,
Heartwarming stirred with kindness,
From The Spirit, will only do.

FEEDING ON GOD'S LOVE

When I look at Your beauty Lord,
I'm feeding on Your love,
My soul stirs within
From Your heavenly touch.

Mother Nature all around me,
I feel her heal and soothe,
A walk in the park
To the glow of Your moon.

Your trees and Your flowers
Turn the sour to sweet,
Feeding on Your love Lord
Supplies all my needs.

I only have to look around,
My cares and fears dismissed,
Your creation's beauty Lord
Are Mother Nature's gifts.

EXCITEMENT IN MY SOUL

There's excitement in my soul Lord,
Some days by chance,
So truly unexpected,
Like the touch of Your hand.

A feeling like no other,
This calm and peace I know,
A joy You bring to me,
That's how Your Spirit flows.

It's beyond my understanding
Why You bless me so,
There's excitement in my soul
Because You, I know.

Thank You Lord for loving me
And the joy You bring,
There's excitement in my soul Lord,
Your love is everything!

A LOVE THAT KNOWS NO END

A love that knows no end
Is from Jesus Christ our Lord,
It never gives up or fades
Because it's you He adores.

He left you His Spirit
Who lives in your heart day and night,
It's there you will hear Him
As He lovingly prompts and guides.

A love that knows no end
Into and beyond Eternity,
Prepares a home in Paradise
For you He bore Calvary.

Each soul is precious
To the immortal Trinity,
A love that knows no end,
Craves for you and me.

THE AUROMA OF CHRIST...
IS IN EVERY GARDEN...

"Praise the Lord, because he is good;
sing praises to his name because he is kind.!"

Psalm 135 : 3

IN SERVICE FOR VICTORY

Thank You for Your servants Lord,
They come with hearts and souls,
So gifted with Your message
For the world to be made whole.

Thank You for Your servants Lord
All over the globe,
They tell Your message to repent
To bring all people home.

They spread Your sacred Word Lord
Bringing trust, hope and faith,
To the corners of the earth Lord
For Your saving mercy and grace.

Thank You for Your servants Lord
Who serve so faithfully,
You charge them with Your power,
They're in service for victory!

KNOW HIM LIKE A BROTHER

Know Him like a brother
Who you rely on and trust,
The one you always run to,
Love Him; you must.

Know Him as your Counsellor
For every need in life,
He wants to share your journey
Because you are precious in His sight.

Know Him as your maker
Who created you,
A spiritual being,
In His image; it's true.

He is your King of Kings,
Creator and Lord of Lords,
The Almighty Heavenly Father,
It's you He adores.

Know Him like a brother,
He loves you so much,
Open your heart
To receive His tender touch.

Born in a humble stable,
On the holiest of nights,
He came to earth just for you
So you could have eternal life.

A LOVE THAT KNOWS NO BOUNDS

A love that knows no bounds
Is one from heaven's realm,
Pure love beyond understanding
To you will unfurl.

No matter what your age
Or how far you've come,
A love that knows no bounds
Is yours when you know God's Son.

Heaven's love so pure
With The Spirit's care,
Your commitment made secure,
In your heart He lives there!

A love that knows no bounds
Will shine with The Spirit's touch,
Like a blazing torch within,
Because He loves you so very much!

AMONGST YOUR BEAUTY LORD

Amongst Your beauty Lord
I feel so complete,
Walking through the park,
Your beauty is what I see.

Mother Nature around me
In colour, size and shape,
The breeze that moves the trees,
My heart it takes.

Your beauty on show Lord
With majesty and grace,
Reaching for the sky,
For us to embrace.

Amongst Your beauty Lord
I feel healing and love,
Everything made by You Lord
From Your heaven above.

PART TWO

"There is one Lord, one faith, one baptism; there is one God and Father of all mankind, who is Lord of all, works through all, and is in all."

Ephesians 4 : 5, 6

NO CARE TOO DEEP...
FOR THE GOD OF MIRACLES...

"God will put his angels in charge of you to protect you wherever you go. They will hold you up with their hands..."

Psalm 91 : 11, 12

ONWARD AS I AM

Onward as I am Lord
In trust and faith,
Your Spirit called me long ago,
I've seen Your precious face.

My life You planned,
My Prince of Peace,
I'm living in You,
I feel so complete.

Onward as I am Lord,
My soul You own,
Your mercy and grace
Will see me home.

Onward as I am Lord,
I still have lessons to learn,
Help me through this process,
For You my glad heart yearns.

Yes, onward as I am Lord,
Through the future ahead,
I know You are with me,
You are my Lord and friend.

TRUST IN THEE

I'm trusting You Lord,
It's all I know to do,
You know me inside out
That's why I trust in You.

Why should I worry?
You are everything to me,
Somedays my life feels empty
But I have to trust in Thee.

I turn to Your Word,
Comfort I find,
Your stories of old,
A revelation in time.

Whatever life might bring,
One message is very clear,
You are always with me
To take my doubts and fears.

Through Your Holy Spirit
A constant and present help,
My faith and trust secure,
For me there's no-one else.

TREASURES IN YOUR LOVE

The treasures in Your love Lord,
Eternal gifts from "Thee",
A never ending supply
For all my needs.

There's no hurt You can't heal,
No broken heart You can't mend,
No wound You can't soothe
From Your love You send.

The treasures in Your love Lord
Shine and glisten in Your light,
A stream of wealth
From Your grace divine.

So precious each one
In Your Holy Name,
The treasures in Your love Lord
Will never change.

ALL IS NOT LOST

All is not lost
When life seems dim,
For the moments you feel weak
Do your best and talk to Him.

You can overcome this challenge,
Look to the other side,
In Jesus you have hope,
Through Him you can survive.

He sent His Holy Spirit
To bring comfort and peace
To those who will come
To His Mercy Seat.

He came to be the Lamb of God,
He took our sin to Calvary
So we could have a home above
He was raised to victory!

All is not lost,
In His grace and mercy we live,
Call on the Saviour today,
Bring your heart to Him.

TEARS WILL SLIP AWAY

I love it Lord when You come to me
When a teardrop is about to fall,
You cup Yor hands around my face
To lovingly catch them all.

When I feel hope slipping away
Or a dream that no longer lives,
My shaky heart says "give up",
It's then Your love You bring.

Sometimes a tear just can't be stopped,
That's healing taking place,
You are there to dry them all
As each one You surely take.

You place them at Your Throne of Gold
Where they just slip away,
Never to be seen again,
I'm in Your arms always.

SURROUND YOURSELF WITH GOD

Surround yourself with God
For heavenly peace,
Hand your cares over
To His Mercy Seat.

There is none other
Who can supply your needs,
His wings of shelter come
When you confide in "Thee".

Challenges will appear
But He will provide
The strength for you in a moment
To move on and survive.

With faith and trust
You can surround yourself with God,
Your spiritual path will open
The Lord God you can lean upon.

CHRIST JESUS THE LIVING GOD... LIVES FOR YOU...

"But have reverence for Christ in your hearts and honor him as Lord..."

1 Peter 3 : 15

PRAY FOR PEACE AND CALM

Praying for God's peace and calm
Can soothe your world,
Through the precious Holy Spirit,
God's mercy and grace upheld.

Bring your cares to His Altar,
He will take them in His Hands,
Ask for His direction,
His will is the plan.

Pray for peace and calm
In all you do,
The Saviour craves your prayers
So He can help you through.

Pray for His peace and calm,
Submit your cares to Him,
Your day will pass so smoothly
You will feel them slowly dim.

LOOK TO THE HOLY SPIRIT

Look to the Holy Spirit,
The perfect answer will come,
God's precious gift
Through Jesus, His only Son.

There's nothing He can't do,
Ask for daily help,
Look to the Holy Spirit,
His presence will be felt.

Look to the Holy Spirit,
Our great Comforter and Shield,
In sorrow and in joy
Through Him we can be healed.

God sent Him through Jesus,
His own Holy Seed,
Seek His daily counsel
In rejoicing and need.

He will bring God's grace and truth,
Restoration you will find,
He will never fail you
In any moment of time.

PERSONAL TIME WITH THE SAVIOUR

Personal time with the Saviour
When we share His Communion Cup,
In those quiet moments,
Our sins are given up.

Personal time with the Saviour,
The choice is yours,
Will you confess to the Saviour?
Because your sin He bore.

In personal time with the Saviour
You can empty your heart,
Trusting He will take care of you,
As you walk your daily path.

He knows the truth,
Every part of you,
Personal time with the Saviour
Is help through and through.

Personal time with the Saviour
Is quiet time alone,
He adores and comforts you,
He will never let you go!

NEVER ALONE

We are never alone Lord
Because Your Spirit lives
Within all believers,
Through Him Your love You give.

Though we may feel differently,
This world tells us so,
Believing in You with trust and faith
We will never be alone.

We are never alone Lord,
In our deepest, darkest hour,
When we are weak in failing health
Your Spirit comes with Your power.

Faith can move mountains
And overcome all ills,
We are never alone Lord,
I know by the way I feel.

LOOK TO THE SAVIOUR

Look to the Saviour
To know how to live,
He was tempted like us
But He never sinned.

When you need a guide
Or a decision to be made,
Look to the Saviour
His answer is on its way.

When you need a shoulder
That will hold many a tear,
Look to the Saviour
He is ever so near.

When you need a miracle
For an aching heart,
Look to the Saviour
He will come with His balm.

Look to the Saviour
In all you do,
You will receive your rewards
That He has waiting for you.

LIVE HIS WORD EVERYDAY

If we live Your Word everyday Lord
Your salvation is at hand,
Our trust and faith would grow
To obey Your commands.

We can live Your Word everyday
With kindness in our hearts,
Your precious Holy Spirit
Will open up a path.

You made us in Your image Lord
And Your Spirit to comfort us,
We can learn Your ways of life
With faith and trust.

Your commandment was to love one another,
This surely can be,
Living Your Word everyday Lord
We can be more like Thee.

We can encounter You Lord,
Your Word forever true,
Miracles are in Your hands
In You we are renewed.

ENCOUNTER GOD...
EVERY DAY...

"God's plan is to make known his secret to his people, this rich and glorious secret which he has for all peoples. And the secret is that Christ is in you, which means that you will share in the glory of God."

Colossians 1 : 27

IN YOUR LOVING CARE

I'm in Your loving care Lord,
No need for me to fear,
Every dawn that rises
My course in life You steer.

Worrying won't change a thing,
This I surely know,
I must trust in my faith,
To me Your love You've shown.

It's true that human nature
Thinks the worst sometimes,
But staying in Your loving care
Will ease the pain that thrives.

Staying in Your loving care
My trust and faith secured,
Through the Holy Spirit
Eternal life assured.

LORD IN YOU

Lord in You
I have strength to overcome,
I have purpose to carry on,
I have Your gift of love.

Lord in You
I have a life to live,
I will find victory
Because of You I can forgive.

Lord in You
I have peace and calm,
Through Your Holy Spirit
I am carried in Your arms.

Lord in You
I have a destiny,
My faith and trust tell me
From the realms of Your Majesty.

Holy Lamb of God
You bring me to my knees,
In You Lord
I have a home in Eternity.

I NEED YOUR DIRECTION LORD

I need Your direction Lord
Every day of my life,
Bless each day to Your will
In Your shining light.

On my own I get lost,
The future I cannot see,
I need Your direction Lord,
You know what's best for me.

Your plans are always perfect Lord
Though I may have to wait,
My lessons are many
As I grow in my faith.

Yes, I need Your direction Lord
Every single day,
Because I bear Your name Lord
You will show me the way.

HIS CALM IS YOUR CALM

His calm is your calm,
You only need to ask,
The answer is simple,
When the day holds many tasks.

The way ahead looks arduous
With hills and valleys deep,
You can overcome them
If His calm you will seek.

He will lay His peace upon you
Through the Spirit's tender care,
His calm will pass over you
Like the coming dawn so fair.

These gifts He will bestow to you
Because He loves you so,
His calm is your calm,
To treasure along life's road.

HIS LOVE WILL SUSTAIN YOU

When you know the Saviour
His Spirit will overflow,
His love will sustain you,
Beyond what you know.

A Baptizing of The Trinity upon your life,
Will surely take place,
Lessons will awaken
To sustain your faith.

Through His Holy Word
Strength you will find,
Confirmation of the Spirit's work
Over all mankind.

Mistakes you will make
But His love will sustain,
Through His mercy and grace
You will carry no blame.

His love will sustain
The heart that will respond,
His voice and direction
You can lean upon.

FIND PEACE WITH THE SAVIOUR

Find peace with the Saviour,
Connect with the Holy One,
Give your cares to Him,
God's only Holy Son.

He's waiting for you to share
What's on your mind,
He craves your attention
To spend with Him some time.

You can always talk things over
With the King of Kings,
Through His Spirit He gave us
You can confess your everything.

Find peace with the Saviour,
In faith and trust you will succeed,
None other will do,
To ask is to receive.

Find peace with the Saviour,
You will encounter God,
Take your smallest care
As Him you lean upon.

You can live in peace with the Saviour
Every day of your life,
Knowing the Holy Spirit
Is the light that shines so bright.

HE CAME TO SERVE...
SO YOU COULD BE A BLESSING...

"Humble yourselves before the Lord,
and he will lift you up."

James 4 : 10

COME INTO HIS SANCTUARY

Come into God's sanctuary
For peace and calm within,
His Holy Spirit will bless you,
Seek your strength in Him.

Come into God's sanctuary
A place of paradise,
Sit at His Mercy Seat
And leave your cares behind.

Put your trust in Him
To resolve those doubts and fears,
Claim His help today
He will dry those falling tears.

Come into His sanctuary
To find solace on your path,
Tranquillity like no other
You will find in His arms.

Divine help is waiting,
You can rise above any task,
Come into His sanctuary,
You only have to ask.

CHALLENGES

Life around us Lord
Brings challenges each day,
But with You as our guide Lord,
You will help us through the maze.

No friend so dear and constant
Can help us like You do,
You crave our prayers each day
So You can help us through.

Our feelings and emotions
Weave a tangled web,
But because You are our Saviour
These challenges can be met.

You equip us with Your mercy
Like a Father to His child,
To help in times of trouble
And ease the pain for a while.

Yes, Lord the challenges of life
Keep on showing up,
But as my personal Saviour
Every day You supply Your love.

SHINING ON THE INSIDE

I'm shining on the inside Lord,
Where Your Spirit lives
Within my heart forever Lord,
Joy and peace You bring.

I'm shining on the inside Lord
With Your love divine
Because You called me long ago,
I'm so glad You are mine.

Your Spirit never leaves me,
You dwell within me always,
You comfort and guide me,
You are my shelter every day.

Yes, I'm shining on the inside Lord
Because of Your love,
I'm so glad You came to me
From Your Throne above.

BRAVE HEARTED

Be of a brave heart
When His Spirit calls to you,
Take that step in faith
For His love so true.

A never ending well
To supply all your needs,
His mercy and grace will equip you
For the challenges you meet.

Time will mature
Your trust over the years,
His goodness is forever,
Your course in life He steers.

Yes, be of a brave heart,
Show a faith to be seen,
You will receive the Saviour's rewards
And sow many seeds.

EMPOWERING LOVE

I pray for Your strength Lord,
To rise above mortality,
Empower me in Your love
So I can be more like Thee.

Your humbling, caring Spirit
Will show me the way,
You pour Your love over me
Because I bear Your Name.

In wisdom and in truth
Your empowering love will remain,
To all who claim You "Saviour",
Sacred is Your Name.

Your empowering love is eternal,
Forever You will remain
Our everlasting Father,
You will never change.

Yes Lord, Your authority is supreme,
In Kingship and Majesty
You reign over the world,
We will rise to victory.

BLESSED BY YOUR SPIRIT

I feel blessed by Your Spirit Lord
From the Holy Trinity,
When I come into Your presence
I am humbled in Thee.

A feeling so real
And natural to me,
Being blessed by The Spirit,
Your greatest gift to me.

Quiet time I share with You
Is strength for my soul,
My faith always growing,
You make me whole.

Thank You for Your blessings Lord
And the gift of The Spirit,
Speaking quietly to my heart
What joy; when I hear Him.

YOUR PRESENCE ALONE

Your presence so divine
And humbling to me,
I think of You Lord
In the realm of Your heavenlies.

In my mind's eye
Your light I see,
Your power and glory
Give me tranquillity.

Your presence alone Lord
Can change the darkest thought,
Your forgiveness from sin
Your Calvary bought.

You alone Lord, our glorious King,
In You we have life,
The kind Your salvation
Makes everything right.

Your presence can bring
The world to its knees,
Your presence alone
Will bring serenity.

On the day we encounter
Your glorious Throne,
Every knee shall bow
When You take us home.

THRONE OF GLORY

Your Throne of Glory Lord,
Eternal joy flows down,
Every knee shall bow,
You are worshipped in a vow.

Your Throne of Glory for mankind,
Our eternal home,
No pain or tears exist
When we call You our own.

Your Throne of Glory, Gracious Lord
Waits in heaven's realm above,
Filled with Your heavenly hosts
Praising You, God's Holy Son.

Your Throne of Glory shines with gold,
In wonder and awe so bright
In time You will reveal
Your glorious Kingdom of Light.

FLOURISHING LOVE

As you grow in the Spirit
Your love will flourish,
He will prompt you to act,
You will know, you will feel it.

So strong, so true,
His Spirit moves
Stirring the soul
To heal and soothe.

Flourishing love
Will spread your wings
To mature your faith to bring others
Closer to Him.

His flourishing love
Knows no bounds,
To reach out and touch
New hearts He has found.

TALK TO THE HOLY SPIRIT

Talk to the Holy Spirit
To truly connect with God,
His power so real
As Him you lean upon.

His love is like no other,
So comforting and sweet,
His magnitude so strong
As to your heart He speaks.

He knows all about you
But still adores you so,
Talk to the Holy Spirit,
Your love will surely grow.

He came down from above
To be our comfort and guide,
He prompts us with His love,
From Him you cannot hide.

He shows the Saviour's love
In many different ways,
Talk to the Holy Spirit,
His love will never fade.

He is the Saviour's gift,
His Word tells us so,
Sent to abide with us
So His blessings can flow.

SALVATION IS AT HAND

For everyone on earth
Salvation is at hand,
Through the Holy One
By obeying His commands.

Through His grace and mercy
You can restore your soul,
A new life for you
In His Word we are told.

The Saviour came to teach us
How we can repent,
By turning from earthly ways,
We can live again.

Salvation is at hand
For His glory and peace,
By believing in the Saviour,
You; He will come to meet.

SPIRIT HOME

Your Throne of Glory Lord
Is my Spirit home,
Built in heaven above
Prepared for hearts You own.

You showed me long ago
How real heaven surely is,
Because Your Spirit lives in me
Your love to me You give.

My Spirit home is light
Because Your glory shines,
Always and forever Lord
You will be mine.

In Your power and Your glory
My Spirit home abides,
And by Your grace and mercy,
I will live by Your side.

Yes, my Spirit home is You Lord
For all eternity,
I will see You on Your Throne,
My King of Kings, Your Majesty!

PART THREE

"Do not be worried and upset," Jesus told them. "Believe in God and believe also in me. There are many rooms in my Father's house, and I am going to prepare a place for you. I would not tell you this if it were not so. And after I go and prepare a place for you, I will come back and take you to myself, so that you will be where I am."

John 14 : 1 - 3

ENCOUNTER GOD'S WAYS...
FIND PEACE IN YOUR LIFE...

"Peace is what I leave with you; it is my own peace that I give you. I do not give it as the world does. Do not be worried and upset; do not be afraid."

John 14 : 27

SO FAITHFUL

Faithful; precious Lord
Is what You are to me;
You never change, You are always the same,
Every day into Eternity.

You love us the same now
As You will into Eternity,
Nothing can stand between us,
Our Deliverer You'll always be.

You forgave our sin
A long time ago,
Help us to repent
So freedom we will know.

We need not have doubts
Or despair in any way,
Because You are so faithful
Our fears You will take away.

We only have to ask
And rely on Your Grace,
Your Holy Spirit will come
To restore our trust and faith!

BECAUSE OF YOU LORD

Because of You Lord, I can love,
Though I may not have met them
Or even know them,
I love; by the love of Heaven.

Because of You Lord, I can forgive,
A hurt that crumbles the heart
And soul, hidden in the depths,
Will rise to victory in You.

Because of You Lord, I have learned tolerance,
I can love with Heaven's love,
Though earthly ways tell me different,
My heart belongs to You!

Because of You Lord, I can walk in Your light,
A light that will never fade,
A light that gives me strength,
And gives me life, day after day.

Because of You Lord,
I have the gift from the Holy Trinity;
The Holy Spirit; and in every believing heart;
I love, because You first loved me.

ALONE WITH MY THOUGHTS

Alone with my thoughts
Can bring comfort and peace
As I think of the Saviour
Who died for me.

Without question I believe
He carried the Cross,
His Ministry on earth
For this purpose was.

My own understanding fails
When I try to believe,
But in trust I accept
What Jesus did for me.

I love Him, I know Him,
The Lamb of God,
His sacrifice given
I can lean upon.

With the Spirit's awakening,
He washed me clean,
My sin gone forever
Because He died for me.

A knowing within
He lives, He lives,
On the Third Day He rose
Eternal Life begins.

HEAVEN'S LANDSCAPE

Heaven's landscape will be pure delight,
I can only imagine the view,
A place where love is manifest
And the soul is made brand new.

The Lord has promised to prepare
Mansions for us all,
A home for His beloved
Who answer the Spirit's call.

Hearts so full of love
Will overflow to the brim,
Living in His presence,
Heavenly choirs in praise will sing.

Hills and valleys so glorious,
Glades to wander and share,
To stroll in the Saviour's glory,
No night time will be there.

The glory of Heaven's landscape
Waits for us all,
One day we will see it clearly
When we hear the Master's call.

GIFT DIVINE

Some days my soul is hungry,
It craves His touch divine,
A need sometimes a mystery
But His Spirit can satisfy.

I can turn to Your Word Lord
That brings You closer still,
My peaceful heart rejoices
Because that need Your Spirit fills.

In trust and faith I'm satisfied
To lean on You all the time,
Though challenges still surface,
You are my gift divine.

The wonder of Your gift Lord,
To all who call You "come",
You bring Your peace and calm Lord,
You are God's Holy Son.

A gift divine You are Lord,
Come share my walk in life,
Master, Lord and Saviour,
I need You by my side.

FULFILMENT

Fulfilment is life
With the Holy Spirit,
A completeness inside
When His voice, you hear it.

Fulfilment is God's love
In the purest form,
From God in His Heaven,
In Him we are reborn.

We can start a new life
Now the heart is refreshed,
Fulfilment is God's love
To help us do our best.

The Lord calls for love,
His commandment for all,
Many lessons required
To answer His call.

Fulfilment in the Spirit
Is a life long journey,
That satisfies the soul
For eternal yearning.

Encounter God today,
Fulfilment you will find,
Through His Holy Spirit
You will know The Divine.

SPEAK TO ME LORD...
LET ME HEAR YOUR VOICE...

"My sheep listen to my voice; I know them, and they follow me. I give them eternal life, and they shall never die. No one can snatch them away from me."

John 10 : 27 - 28

AWAKENING OF THE SPIRIT

The awakening of the Spirit
Stirs my soul,
By one so Holy
Who makes me whole.

His love is the reason
I see so clearly,
How He loves and guides me
In my life so dearly.

He gives me calm and peace
When anxious I become,
He soothes my weary mind
When I ask for His healing balm.

The awakening of His Spirit
Is the gift from the Trinity,
Changes lives forever,
This gift He gave to me.

IN LOVE WITH JESUS

Being in love with Jesus
Can take many years to grow,
Changing our ways is paramount
As the Spirit in time will show.

It's a matter of feeding and drinking
To nourish the heart and soul,
Reading His Word is food for the heart
And prayer the wine for the soul.

Carrying the fruits of the Spirit,
Will mature the heart in time,
As we wander along the journey
With God's Word the clinging vine.

Your heart will feel content
Because you acted in your faith,
While your soul is at peace,
Restoration takes place.

Challenges may rise
But the Counsellor is at hand,
Present to the Master,
The only one who understands.

No problem too big
As His will comes to pass,
Left in His hands,
You only have to ask!

HIS MIRACLES HAPPEN TODAY

His miracles happen today
As in days of old,
Still wielding His precious hand
In silence to behold.

An act done in His Name
To help someone else,
Brings pleasure to His heart
Because His love we felt.

Every day there's a need
Either big or small,
His miracles happen today
A prayer will bring His call.

Encounter God through prayer,
An earnest longing of the heart,
Only if it is His will
Can this come to pass.

God's miracles happen today,
Of that there is no doubt,
Show His love you carry
By helping someone out.

PEACE FOR REST

The Saviour's peace for rest
After the chores of yesterday,
Tomorrow is on the horizon,
With His plan on the way.

Nought can change yesterday,
Look for the Saviour's peace,
Place all cares in His hands,
Believe those challenges will cease.

Though doubts and fears may rise,
Don't let them take control,
Send them in prayer to Jesus,
In His hands they will be resolved.

Look to the Saviour's peace for rest,
Let today's sunshine take hold,
He sent you His Holy Spirit,
His joy is truth to behold.

OPEN TO THE SPIRIT

Open to the Spirit
To receive God's love,
He will comfort and guide you
Through His Holy Son.

Open to the Spirit
For His sweet love to grow
Into your life forever,
That I surely know.

Open to the Spirit
So you will have perfect peace,
His strength you can call on
When you have the need.

Yes, open to the Spirit
To receive His love divine,
Always and forever
He will make you shine.

MY SOUL'S DELIGHT

My soul's delight, the Holy Spirit,
    So precious and divine,
    He alone brings Jesus' love,
    In light and love He shines.

In wonder and awe the Spirit lives,
    That words just can't explain,
    The majesty of God's own Son
    From heaven to earth He came.

My soul's delight is the heavenlies,
    A realm only God can make,
    One day we will be shown
    How and when they were made.

For now I hear the Spirit's call,
Tenderly and gently He prompts,
His love brings awe and wonder,
    My heart can only respond!

PART FOUR

"The traitor had given the crowd a signal:
"The man I kiss is the one you want. Arrest him
and take him away under guard." As soon as Judas
arrived, he went up to Jesus and said, "Teacher!"
and kissed him. So they arrested Jesus and held him tight."

Mark 14 : 44 - 46

GIVE HIM YOUR HEART...
HE GAVE YOU HIS LIFE...

"With a loud cry Jesus died.
The curtain hanging in the Temple
was torn in two, from top to bottom."

Mark 15 : 37 - 38

WORSHIP AND SONG

In the Upper Room, so sacred,
They shared in the Bread and the Wine,
Chosen by the Saviour,
A Sacrament to be remembered through time.

The Bread and the Wine
Represented His body and His blood,
Given for mankind
Upon the cruel Cross.

In private they ate together
Not realizing the truth,
One would betray the Master
To bring prophesy true.

Finally He led them
To Gethsemane to pray,
Grief overwhelmed Him
But the Father's will He obeyed.

In the dark of night,
Worship and song a memory,
His last teaching; The Sacraments,
In remembrance for Thee.

HEAVEN'S KEY

The Cross; so sacred and Holy
Held the King of Kings,
A sacrifice predestined
Would become Heaven's Key.

A figure so powerful
Could calm an angry storm,
He spoke and the sea fell silent,
His voice called the dawn.

The Cross; a symbol of truth,
Bought eternal life,
Divine love in great magnitude
Would be our eternal light.

The Cross; held humanity
Upon God's Holy Son,
He paid the price of salvation
So forgiven we could become.

The Cross; is Heaven's Key,
The owner is Christ the Lord,
Through the gift of The Holy Spirit
The Trinity we will adore.

REACHING ARMS

Precious arms that spanned the Cross,
Open wide for all mankind,
His passion for you drove Him there,
One for many would give His life.

His hands bore the nails
And a spear pierced His side,
Blood and water poured out
For you and I.

The cost is so priceless,
No earthly coin could buy,
His arms can always reach you,
His Redemption came from on high.

He is the one and only
Whose arms are always open wide,
No matter who you are,
For you, He died.

Arms that will always reach for you
Will be for Eternity,
He gave His life for you,
In His arms you always will be.

Calvary couldn't stop Him,
Through the agony He saw His Throne,
He knew His Kingdom was waiting
And His Father to welcome Him home.

PRAISE THE LIVING GOD… FOREVER AND EVER…

"Suddenly there was a violent earthquake; an angel of
the Lord came down from heaven, rolled the stone away, and sat on
it. His appearance was like lightning, and his clothes were
white as snow. The guards were so afraid that they trembled and
became like dead men. The angel spoke to the women.
"You must not be afraid," he said. "I know you are looking
for Jesus, who was crucified. He is not here; he has been raised,
just as he said. Come here and see the place where he was lying."

Matthew 28 : 2 - 6

THE GLORY OF GOD'S POWER

The dawn brought such joy,
It revealed an empty grave,
The Saviour found in the garden,
Grave clothes thrown away.

The glory of God's power
Raised Jesus from the grave,
In the garden He was found,
The stone was rolled away.

Victory over death,
Seen this Easter Day,
The glory of God's power
Forever an empty grave.

The glory of God's power
Sent the Spirit's flame,
To be with us on earth
Blessed is His Name.

Christ now walks the halls of Heaven,
Triumphant is His Name,
Preparing our home in Paradise,
His glory shall remain.

GLORIOUS EASTER DAY

Glorious Easter Day,
The Stone was rolled away,
He lives, He lives today,
Death was erased.

After the agony of the Cross,
He laid in the Tomb,
Anointed with oils
To heal His wounds.

On the Third Day
His glory was revealed,
The Tomb now empty,
He lives this Easter Day.

Glorious Easter Day,
He lives, He lives forever,
Grave now wide open,
Angels roar in Heaven.

Glorious Easter Day,
King of Kings raised to life,
He lives forever more
Angels sing with pure delight.

THE HOLIEST OF NIGHTS...
CHRIST IS BORN IN THE MANGER...

"This very day in David's town your Saviour was
born - Christ the Lord! And this is what will prove it to you:
You will find a baby wrapped in cloths and lying in a manger."

Luke 2 : 11 - 12

GOD'S FAVOUR POURED OUT

Obedient servant of God,
By the Holy Spirit she conceived,
The Mother of the Saviour
So reverent, so gracious, so serene.

What favour shone upon her,
To be chosen by God,
The angel came in God's glory
To deliver the news from above.

She accepted obediently,
The favour of God,
She visited her cousin Elizabeth
Who was expecting her child, John.

Together they worshipped God,
Great news to behold,
God's favour poured out
As the months came along.

Joseph took Mary to Bethlehem
For the Census of the land,
There the Saviour was born
As God had planned.

God's favour poured out
On this gentle soul,
So worthy, so beloved,
As the Scriptures foretold.

HOLY, HOLY NIGHT

The wonder and the glory
Christ the Saviour is born,
Over two thousand years on
He is adored.

The Messiah's message
Is still told today,
Mary conceived by the Spirit,
Glory, glory, on Christmas Day.

We read in His Word
How the angels came down,
To herald His birth,
Their message so profound.

Quietly He was born,
The Manger revealed,
The Shepherds bowed down,
Lambs and calves came to kneel.

The Magi arrived following
The Star overhead,
Bringing gifts so poignant
For His Ministry ahead.

What glory rang out
On that Holy, Holy night,
In the hills of Bethlehem,
The Saviour has arrived.

A LOVE SO REAL

A love so real
Came that Holy Night,
On the eve of Christmas
A Star shone bright.

Heavenly angels came down
In unison they sang,
Glorious praises to God,
Holy voices rang.

A sight to behold,
Shepherds in the fields,
Went to behold the Messiah,
So lowly they kneeled.

The Magi brought gifts
In worship bowed down,
Kings from the East
Wore robes and crowns.

Frankincense, Myrrh and Gold
They presented to Him,
In majesty and awe
They adored the Messiah King.

ALWAYS AND FOREVER

Always and forever Lord
You will be the great "I Am",
Truth and grace Your stronghold
Because You are the Holy Lamb.

You were born in a Stable
On the holiest of nights,
Always and forever Lord
You wear the Crown of Life.

Always and forever Lord
You will love the whole wide world,
Your mission is to save us,
Your message we must tell.

Always and forever Lord
You are the Risen Christ,
Your hands and feet bore the nails
So we could have eternal life.

You gave us Your Holy Spirit,
Holy is Your Name,
Always and forever Lord
Blessed: You remain!

ALSO BY CLAIRE GROSE

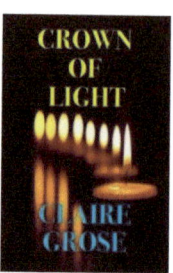
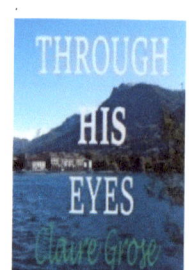

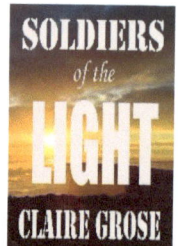
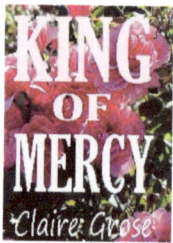

ABOUT THE AUTHOR

Claire worked as a Government Public Servant in the Lands Department, Adelaide, South Australia until she married and became a mother of two boys.

She later returned to the work force during which time she gained a "Living Hope" Phone Counselling certificate which influenced her need to help others.

Through this and personal experience she found herself inspired by God's love to put pen to paper.

PHOTO CREDITS

COVER PHOTO: Canola Crop; Daveyston; S.A. - Claire Grose

Page 2: Mt Titles; Switzerland. – Michael and Andrea
Page 12: Obi Obi ; Qld. – Carol and Dennis
Page 24: Dovecoat; S.A. – Karen
Page 31: Landmark, Snaefellsness Peninsula; Iceland - Kate
Page 39: Garden Feature; S.A. - Karen and Jeff
Page 47: Ornamental Vines; S.A. - Karen and Jeff
Page 55: Vineyard, Charleston; S.A. - Claire Grose
Page 70: Witta Hinterland; Qld. – Claire Grose
Page 78: Yucca flowering buds; Qld. – Carol and Dennis
Page 87: Salisbury Uniting Church Cross; S.A. – Claire Grose
Page 92: Salisbury Uniting Church Cross; S.A. – Claire Grose
Page 96: Salisbury Uniting Church; S.A. – Claire Grose

ENCOUNTER GOD

www.ingramcontent.com/pod-product-compliance
Lightning Source LLC
Chambersburg PA
CBHW042043290426
44109CB00001B/13